Fossil Fuels

by Tracy Vonder Brink

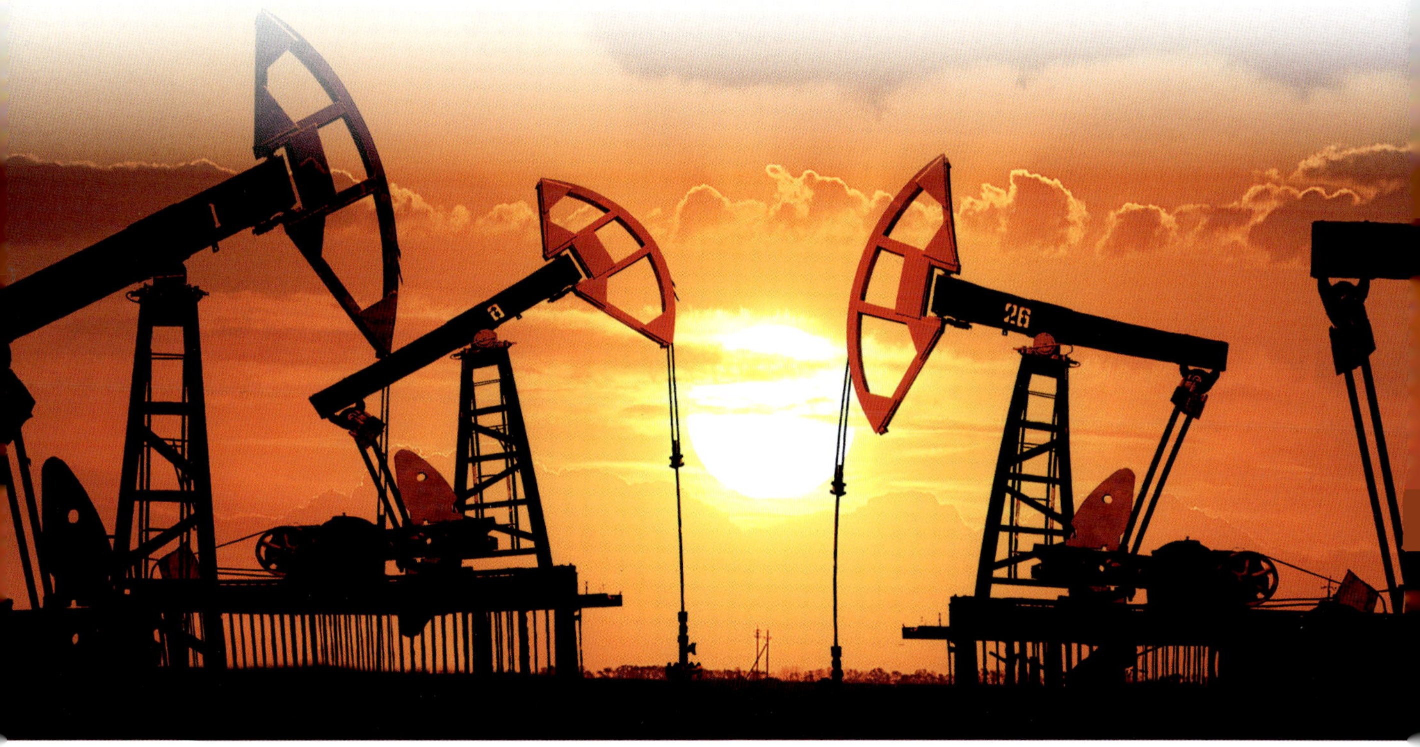

A Crabtree Crown Book

School-to-Home Support for Caregivers and Teachers

This appealing book is designed to teach students about core subject areas. Students will build upon what they already know about the subject, and engage in topics that they want to learn more about. Here are a few guiding questions to help readers build their comprehension skills. Possible answers appear here in red.

Before Reading:

What do I know about fossil fuels?

- *I know fuel makes energy.*
- *I know fuel runs cars.*

What do I want to learn about this topic?

- *I want to know about the different kinds of fossil fuels.*
- *I want to learn how fossil fuels work.*

During Reading:

I'm curious to know...

- *I'm curious to know where gasoline comes from.*
- *I'm curious to know how fossil fuels affect climate change.*

How is this like something I already know?

- *I know gasoline is used in cars.*
- *I know fossil fuels give off carbon dioxide when they are burned.*

After Reading:

What was the author trying to teach me?

- *The author was trying to teach me what fossil fuels are.*
- *The author was trying to teach me why we need to replace fossil fuels.*

How did the photographs and captions help me understand more?

- *The photographs helped me understand where fossil fuels come from.*
- *The captions gave me extra information.*

Table of Contents

Chapter 1
Energy and Fuel 4

Chapter 2
What Is Oil? 11

Chapter 3
What Is Coal? 14

Chapter 4
What Is Natural Gas? 16

Chapter 5
Powering a City 18

Chapter 6
Challenges of Fossil Fuels 22

Chapter 7
The Future of Fossil Fuels 27

Glossary 30

Index 31

Comprehension Questions 31

About the Author 32

Chapter 1: Energy and Fuel

We need energy for everything we do. Energy heats our homes. Our bodies use it to live. It fuels our cars. But what is energy?

In science, work is energy moving from one object to another. Your feet pushing against your bike's pedals are doing work that makes the bike move.

Energy is the ability to do work or to make something happen. Energy is everywhere. It comes in different forms. Heat, light, and sound are all forms of energy. The lights in your home use electrical energy.

Transforming Energy

Energy can be transformed, or changed, from one form to another. Energy changes forms when it is used to make something happen. Wood has energy locked inside it. Burning the wood changes its energy into heat and light.

Heat and light are two forms of energy.

A fuel is something that is changed in some way to produce energy. Wood is a fuel because burning it releases heat and light. Food is fuel for your body. Your body breaks down what you eat and uses it as energy.

Fossil Fuels

Most fossil fuels formed during the Carboniferous Period. No dinosaurs lived during this time. They lived nearly a hundred million years later.

We use fuels to make heat and power. Today, most of our heat and power comes from fossil fuels. Most fossil fuels formed from ancient plants beginning around 300 million years ago. How did ancient plants become today's fuels?

Most of the coal on Earth began as trees from the Carboniferous Period.

Millions of years ago, swamps and oceans covered Earth. When plants and other creatures died there, their remains sank to the bottom. They were buried under layers of sand, clay, and other **minerals**.

Plants Become Power

Plants store energy as they grow and live. Over millions of years, heat and pressure changed ancient plants' remains into materials that could be used as sources of fuel. These are known as fossil fuels. These fuels make good power sources because they release a lot of energy when burned. Oil, coal, and natural gas are all fossil fuels.

Chapter 2: What Is Oil?

A pumpjack moves up and down to pump oil from the ground.

Venezuela has the most oil in the world. About 18 percent of the world's known oil is in Venezuela.

Oil is a black liquid. It began as tiny plants and other creatures that lived in oceans. Oil is found underground in **reservoirs**. Wells are drilled into the reservoir, and the oil is pumped out. Then the oil goes to a **refinery** where it is heated.

How We Use Oil

Heating oil at the refinery helps separate it into different parts. Some parts become gasoline, diesel, or jet fuel. Others are used in plastics. Thousands of different products are made from oil.

The state of Texas has the most oil refineries in the United States.

Oil became a popular energy source in the 1800s. People burned it in lamps to light their homes.

Fuels such as gasoline are burned to power cars, trucks, planes, and other vehicles. Items made from plastic are all around us. Oil is even used to make crayons.

Chapter 3: What Is Coal?

The United States has the most coal in the world. About 25 percent of the world's known coal is in the United States.

Coal looks like a black rock. It began as woody plants and trees in swamps. Most coal is buried underground. If it is near the surface, machines scrape off the dirt and other rocks and dig it up. If it is deep underground, tunnels called mine shafts are used to reach it. Some may be 1,000 feet (305 m) deep.

People have been burning coal to heat their homes and cook their food for thousands of years. In the 1800s, engines that used coal were invented. Today, coal burned in power plants creates electricity.

Coal-powered engines, machines, and factories led to the Industrial Revolution. This period changed the way goods were made, and led to the growth of cities.

Chapter 4: What Is Natural Gas?

Russia has the largest amount of natural gas in the world. About 24 percent of the world's known natural gas is in Russia.

Natural gas has no color and is lighter than air. Like oil, it began as tiny plants and other creatures in the ocean. It often formed at the same time as oil, so natural gas may be found in pockets above oil. Natural gas may also be found in its own reservoir. To get natural gas, wells are drilled into the reservoir, and the gas flows through a pipe to the surface.

Natural gas is stored in large tanks.

How We Use Natural Gas

Natural gas was first burned in streetlamps in the 1800s. Today, many home heating systems burn natural gas for heat. Some stoves and dryers use it. Natural gas also generates electricity in some power plants.

Chapter 5: Powering a City

Making Electricity

In a coal power plant, the heat from burning coal boils water like a giant teakettle. The boiling water releases steam. The heat from burning natural gas also boils water in some power plants. In other natural gas power plants, burning natural gas releases hot gases.

Fuel is burned to turn steam turbines like this one.

A generator is a machine that turns motion into electricity.

In all of these power plants, either the steam or the hot gas pushes against blades connected to a generator. The blades turn, and the generator makes electricity.

Moving Electricity

The electricity generated by power plants travels through power lines to a **substation**. The substation changes the electricity into a form that can be sent to a **power grid**. All sources of electricity feed into the same power grids.

Electricity in a power grid may come from both fossil fuels and other energy sources.

Electrical power may flow through several different substations before it reaches a home or business.

Smaller substations carry the electricity to towns and cities. Power lines above or below the ground connect them. Electricity flows from the substation into homes, businesses, streetlights, and more.

Chapter 6: Challenges of Fossil Fuels

Fossil fuels take millions of years to form. They are nonrenewable resources. This means that they cannot be replaced if we use them up. The world's known **reserves** of oil and natural gas could run out within about 50 years, and coal within about 115 years.

Climate Change

Fossil fuels give off **carbon dioxide** when burned. Carbon dioxide collects in a layer around Earth. This layer traps heat and warms the planet. As Earth becomes warmer, its **climate** changes.

Earth's climate has changed many times, but burning fossil fuels is changing it faster than ever before. Higher temperatures and less rain mean less water for people and for crops. Extreme weather and more forest fires may happen. Climate change harms people and animals.

Polar bears are one of the animals harmed by climate change. Polar bears live and hunt on sea ice. Warmer temperatures melt the ice they need to survive.

Pollution

Burning fossil fuels also releases **nitrogen** into the air. Too much nitrogen creates **smog** and makes it harder for people to breathe. The extra nitrogen can also combine with rain, which then harms some bodies of water.

Oil Spills

Oil spills harm the oceans. In 2010, the largest oil spill in history was caused by an explosion on the Deepwater Horizon drilling rig in the Gulf of Mexico. The spill dumped more than 200 million gallons (757 million liters) of oil into the water, enough to fill about 300 swimming pools. Birds, fish, dolphins, and many other sea animals died. Oil from the accident washed up on shores and beaches.

Oil spilled from the Deepwater Horizon stretched over 57,500 square miles (149,000 square km) of water.

Chapter 7: The Future of Fossil Fuels

Fossil fuels supply 84 percent of the world's energy. China uses the most coal, and the United States uses the most oil and natural gas. Many of the world's current power plants are made to run on fossil fuels. They are a powerful source of energy, but fossil fuels change Earth's climate. They will also run out.

Changing for the Future

Many countries are working to change how we use fossil fuels. **Alternative** energy sources such as solar power will not run out and do not give off carbon dioxide. Planting more trees would help remove carbon dioxide from the air.

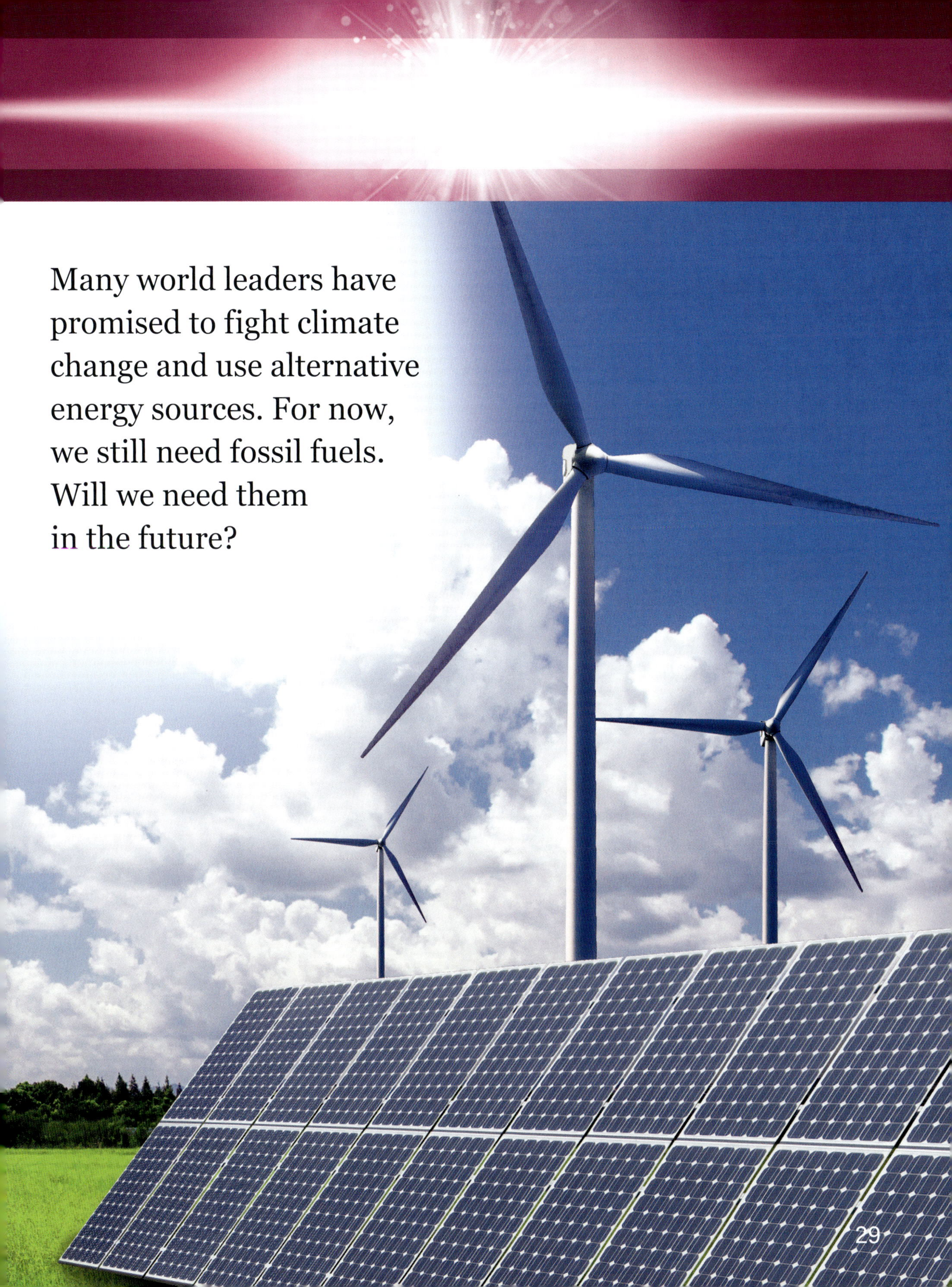

Many world leaders have promised to fight climate change and use alternative energy sources. For now, we still need fossil fuels. Will we need them in the future?

Glossary

alternative (ahl-TUR-nuh-tive): Something that may be chosen instead of something else

carbon dioxide (CAR-bun dye-OX-ide): A gas that is produced when people or animals breathe out or when certain fuels are burned

climate (KLEYE-muht): The usual weather conditions of a particular place

minerals (MIH-nuh-rlz): Solid substances that are naturally formed under the ground

nitrogen (NEYE-tr-jn): A colorless, odorless chemical that makes up a large part of Earth's atmosphere

power grid (PAU-ur GRID): A connected system for delivering electrical power from power plants to homes and businesses

refinery (ruh-FEYE-nr-ee): A facility where raw materials are changed into valuable substances

reserves (ruh-ZURVZ): Supplies of something that are stored for future use

reservoirs (REH-zr-vwahrz): Rock formations that hold oil and natural gas

smog (SMAWG): A type of air pollution that is caused by fog mixed with smoke

substation (SUHB-stay-shn): Equipment that makes electricity usable for people

Index

carbon dioxide 23, 28
climate 23-24, 27, 29
coal 8, 10, 14-15, 18, 22, 27
electricity 15, 17-19, 20-21
gasoline 12-13
natural gas 10, 16-19, 22, 27
oil 10-13, 16, 18, 22, 26-27
power plant(s) 15, 17-21, 27
refinery 11-12
reservoir(s) 11, 16

Comprehension Questions

1. Which of these is a fossil fuel?
   a. Carbon dioxide
   b. Nitrogen
   c. Natural gas
2. Which of these is made from oil?
   a. Glass
   b. Plastic
   c. Cardboard
3. Which country uses the most coal?
   a. United States
   b. China
   c. Venezuela
4. True or False: Nonrenewable energy sources can be replaced.
5. True or False: Fossil fuels supply most of the world's energy.

Comprehension questions answer key: 1. c 2. b 3. b 4. False 5. True

About the Author

Tracy Vonder Brink loves true stories and facts. She has written more than 20 books for kids and is a contributing editor for three children's science magazines. Tracy lives in Cincinnati, Ohio, with her husband, two daughters, and two rescue dogs.

Written by: Tracy Vonder Brink
Designed by: Jennifer Bowers
Series Development: James Earley
Proofreader: Melissa Boyce
Educational Consultant: Marie Lemke M.Ed.
Print Coordinator: Katherine Berti

Photographs: cover ©2012 yevgeniy11/Shutterstock, ©R2D2/Shutterstock; p.4 ©2021 Lin Xiu Xiu/Shutterstock; p.5 ©2015 Africa Studio/Shutterstock; p.6 ©2020 Natalia Leinonen/Shutterstock; p.7 ©2016 Tatjana Baibakova/Shutterstock; p.8 ©2016 Marbury/Shutterstock; p.9 ©BlueRingMedia/Shutterstock; p.10 ©2013 huyangshu/Shutterstock; p.11 ©2016 PhotoStock10/Shutterstock, ©2019 Negro Elkha/Shutterstock; p.12 ©2013 KawinSam/Shutterstock; p.13 ©2018 roopankit/Shutterstock; p.14 ©2015 lusia83/Shutterstock, ©2020 Sunshine Seeds/Shutterstock; p.15 ©2013 jctabb/Shutterstock; p.16 ©2017 tonton/Shutterstock; p.17 ©2016 Marian Weyo/Shutterstock; p.18 ©2018 RobynCharnley/Shutterstock; p.19 ©2013 CoolKengzz/Shutterstock; p.20-21 ©2017 Jenson/Shutterstock; p.22 ©2019 Negro Elkha/Shutterstock, ©2006 Anton Bryksin/Shutterstock, ©2013 Adam J/Shutterstock; p.23 ©2017 leolintang/Shutterstock; p.24 ©2014 FloridaStock/Shutterstock; p.25 ©2019 paradoo/Shutterstock; p.26 ©2020 Colin Seddon/Shutterstock, ©2019 Elliott Cowand Jr/Shutterstock; p.27 ©2018 Olivier Le Moal/Shutterstock; p.28-29 ©2018 xujun/Shutterstock

Library and Archives Canada Cataloguing in Publication

Available at the Library and Archives Canada

Library of Congress Cataloging-in-Publication Data

Available at the Library of Congress

Crabtree Publishing Company

www.crabtreebooks.com 1-800-387-7650

Published in the United States
Crabtree Publishing
347 Fifth Avenue
Suite 1402-145
New York, NY, 10016

Published in Canada
Crabtree Publishing
616 Welland Ave.
St. Catharines, ON
L2M 5V6

Printed in the U.S.A./072022/CG20220201